BUTTERFLIES AND MOTHS

A TRUE BOOK

by

Larry Dane Brimner

Children's Press®
A Division of Grolier Publishing

New York London Hong Kong Sydney
Danbury, Connecticut

Tiger moth,
South America

Subject Consultant
Jeffrey Hahn
*Associate Professor
University of Minnesota
Extension Service
Department of Entomology*

Reading Consultant
Linda Cornwell
*Coordinator of School Quality
and Professional Improvement
Indiana State Teachers
Association*

Author's Dedication
*For kids everywhere
who love bugs*

*The photo on the cover shows
a swallowtail butterfly and
chrysalis. The photo on the
title page shows a morpho
butterfly in Brazil.*

Library of Congress Cataloging-in-Publication Data

Brimner, Larry Dane.
    Butterflies and moths / by Larry Dane Brimner.
        p.   cm. — (A true book)
    Includes bibliographical references and index.
    Summary: Describes the physical characteristics, behavior, and life
cycle of butterflies and moths.
    ISBN 0-516-21162-5 (lib. bdg.)   0-516-26756-6 (pbk.)
    1. Lepidoptera—Juvenile literature.   [1. Butterflies. 2. Moths.]
I. Title. II. Series.
QL544.2.B725   1999
595.78—dc21   99-13839
                                                          CIP
                                                          AC

Contents

Most butterflies are active during the day.

By Day and by Night

Under the warm summer sun, butterflies flutter from flower to flower. Some of their colors and patterns are as brilliant as the stained-glass windows of a church.

Butterflies are among the world's most beautiful insects. Many people even plant "butterfly gardens" to attract them.

Most moths are active at night.

When the sun goes down, the butterflies rest. Now, moths flutter around the glow of streetlights. Moths are not usually as colorful as their butterfly cousins. But their quiet patterns and softer colors allow them to rest unseen all day when butterflies are out and about.

Soft coloring helps these moths rest unseen during the day.

Butterflies and moths live all over the world, except in the coldest parts. There are 12,000 to 15,000 different kinds, or species, of butter-flies, and 150,000 to 250,000 species of moths. They vary greatly in size. The midget moth and western pygmy blue butterfly measure only about 1/8 inch (0.3 cm) from wing tip to wing tip. The atlas moth and Queen Alexandra's birdwing butterfly are as big

The hairstreak butterfly (left) is one of the smaller butterflies of the world. The atlas moth (below) can have a wingspan of 11 inches (28 cm).

as birds! These giants have wingspans of about 11 inches (27.5 cm).

Wings of Scales

Butterflies and moths belong to the same group of insects. The scientific name for this group is *Lepidoptera*, which means "scaly winged." This is a good name because these insects' wings are covered with tiny, powdery scales.

Butterflies (left) and moths (below) belong to the same group of insects.

Have you ever touched the wings of a butterfly or moth? Did you find a fine powder left behind on your fingers? That powder was really scales from the wings.

A butterfly (above) and a close-up view of the scales on its wings (right)

The top sides and undersides of the wings of the same butterfly

These scales give the wings their beautiful patterns and bright colors. These patterns and colors help the insects

13

identify one another. Often, the undersides of the wings are completely different from the tops.

Sometimes the patterns and colors are dull and uninteresting. This is especially true of moths. But this helps them to hide from enemies— especially birds.

A few butterflies are sometimes colorful and sometimes drab. They flash colorful patterns when they fly. When

This moth's colors help it blend into its surroundings.

they are resting, however, the plain undersides of their wings provide camouflage.

Staying Alive

Can you spot the moth?

Butterflies and moths have various ways of protecting themselves from their enemies. Many moths have dull colors that help them blend in with the bark of trees. Camouflage is their way of fooling their enemies.

The owl butterfly has two giant eyespots on its wings. They aren't real eyes, but they scare away enemies.

Some butterflies mimic other butterflies. Birds avoid eating Monarch butterflies because they taste awful. The viceroy butterfly mimics the Monarch butterfly by looking almost exactly like it. This fools hungry birds. Can you tell which butterfly is which?

Owl butterfly

Viceroy butterfly

Monarch butterfly

Feet that Taste

Like all insects, butterflies and moths have six legs. They also have a hard shell, called an exoskeleton, that protects their body. They don't have a skeleton on the inside, like humans do. The exoskeleton is divided into three sections: the head, thorax, and abdomen.

Great spangled fritillary butterfly

Head
Thorax
Abdomen

Moths and butterflies have
large compound eyes on
each side of their head. Each

Close-up of a butterfly's compound eyes

compound eye is made up of thousands of lenses, or facets. Each lens is like a separate eye. These compound eyes help butterflies and moths see all around them.

Butterflies and moths have a special kind of tongue called a proboscis. They use this proboscis like a straw to drink nectar, a sweet liquid that flowers make.

Some of these insects have very long proboscises that can reach deep into flowers. The

A hawkmoth dipping its proboscis into a flower

Close-up of
a birdwing
butterfly's
proboscis

proboscis of the Darwin's hawkmoth is longer than its body!
Butterflies and moths curl up
their proboscises when they are
not using them.

Butterflies and moths have
antennae, or feelers, with tiny
holes in them that admit smells.

Most butterflies have slight knobs at the end of their antennae (above). Most moths have feathery-looking antennae (right).

This helps the insects find food in flowers. It also helps them find mates. The antennae of most butterflies have slight knobs at the ends. A moth's antennae are usually feathery.

The thorax is where all the action is. Three pairs of legs and the insect's wings are attached to the thorax.

A butterfly's feet are used for more than just walking. Butterflies can taste with their feet, so they know right away when they have landed on a sweet flower.

The abdomen is the third section. It holds the body parts that digest food, as well as the parts needed for making and laying eggs.

Butterflies "taste" flowers with their feet.

Changes

Female butterflies and moths produce a chemical substance called pheromone when they are ready to mate. This is a special scent that attracts males of the same species— sometimes from miles away. The male then flies to the female and they flutter around

Copper butterflies mating

each other for a while. After they mate, the male flies away and the female lays eggs.

A female butterfly or moth lays anywhere from fifty to a thousand eggs after she has mated. She is careful to lay her eggs in just the right place. If her young will eat only certain kinds of plants when they hatch, she lays her eggs on those plants.

The eggs are tiny—about the size of the head of a pin. Some will hatch, but many will be eaten by other insects and animals. Those that do hatch won't look anything like their parents. They will be caterpillars.

Caterpillars hatching

Caterpillars spend most of their time eating (left). This Monarch caterpillar (below) has just molted its skin.

Eating and growing are what caterpillars do best. As its body grows, the caterpillar's skin becomes too tight, so it splits out of the old skin. This is called molting. A caterpillar molts several times as it grows. Each time it molts, it is bigger than it was before.

It is dangerous being a caterpillar. Mammals, birds, and lizards like to eat them.

Some caterpillars have scary-looking spikes.

Different caterpillars have different ways of protecting themselves. Some disguise themselves. They might look like small snakes. Others have sharp horns on their bodies. Still others can spit in their enemy's face or blast them with a nasty-smelling spray.

Caterpillars have six pairs of eyes, but they cannot see very well. Mostly, they rely on their antennae to feel their way along.

The metamorphosis of a Monarch butterfly

After many weeks of eating and growing, a caterpillar is ready for the next stage of life. It stops eating and spins a button of silk that holds it firmly to a plant stem. Then it sheds its skin once more and changes into a pupa, also called a chrysalis. The pupa is surrounded by a

hard shell. Inside the shell, the pupa changes into a butterfly or moth. For some kinds of caterpillars, this change, or metamorphosis, takes only a week or two. For others, it takes a whole winter.

Some moths spin cocoons to protect the pupa as it

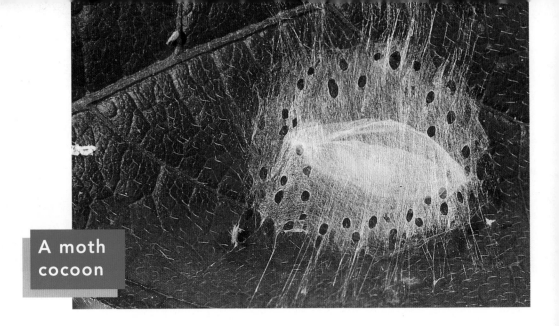

A moth cocoon

changes into an adult moth. Very few butterflies spin cocoons.

Eventually, the shell of the pupa splits open and a new butterfly or moth wriggles out. It is wet and crumpled. Its wings must unfold and dry out. In about an hour, it is ready to fly. And the cycle of life begins again.

Butterfly or Moth?

How can you tell a butterfly from a moth?

• Butterflies tend to be active during the day; most moths are active at night.

• Butterflies are usually more brightly colored than moths, but not always.

• Most butterflies hold their wings up when they are resting; moths usually spread their wings out while resting.

Seven different moths resting on a tree trunk

Fly Away Home

Most butterflies sleep, or hibernate, when winter comes. A few types of butterflies fly, or migrate, amazing distances to warmer places. Monarch butterflies, for example, migrate from the eastern United States and Canada to Mexico or California—a

Monarch butterflies
gathering to migrate

distance of 2,000 miles
(3,219 km) or more. Often,
they glide on air currents—
rivers of air high in the sky.

In the spring, Monarch butterflies fly north again. The females lay their eggs along the way. Now they have reached their goal and have done what was expected of them—producing a new generation of butterflies. Their lives will soon end. When the new generation of Monarchs becomes adult in the late summer and fall, they will make the journey to Mexico or California for the winter.

Monarch butterflies in
California in the winter

Useful Insects

Not many people appreciate hungry caterpillars. They can damage crops that farmers plant. They can destroy the flowers that gardeners enjoy. Sometimes farmers and gardeners use pesticides to kill them. But caterpillars are an important food for many birds and other animals.

Caterpillars are an important food for certain birds and other animals.

Butterflies and moths play an important part in nature. As they flutter from flower to flower sipping nectar, they also spread pollen—just like bees. Pollen is a powdery substance inside flowers that helps new plants to grow.

As adults, butterflies and moths are also important food for many birds, mammals, and other animals. Their beauty and grace are only part of what they do for the world.

Zebra butterflies

To Find Out More

Here are some additional resources to help you learn more about butterflies and moths:

 **Books**

Delafosse, Claude. **Butterflies.** Scholastic Trade, 1997.

Feltwell, John. **Eyewitness Explorers: Butterflies and Moths.** Dorling Kindersley, Ltd., 1993.

Julivert, Maria Angels. **The Fascinating World of Butterflies and Moths.** Barron's Juveniles, 1993.

Mudd, Maria M. **The Butterfly.** Stewart, Tabori & Chang, 1991.

Pascoe, Elaine. **Nature Close-up: Butterflies and Moths.** Blackbirch Press, 1997.

Still, John. **Eyewitness Juniors: Amazing Butterflies and Moths.** Alfred A. Knopf, 1991.

Organizations and Online Sites

The Butterfly Zone
http://www.butterflies.com/

Learn about different types of butterflies and what will attract them to your home garden.

Children's Butterfly Site
http://www.mesc.usgs.gov/ butterfly/butterfly.html

A very informative site that answers many common questions about butterflies and moths. Also includes coloring pages showing the life cycle of the Monarch.

Monarch Watch
http://www.monarcwatch.org/

Follow the migration of the Monarch butterfly and learn about why they migrate. Also provides information about raising Monarchs at home or in a classroom, as well as tips on starting a butterfly garden.

North American Butterfly Association
http://www.naba.org/

A non-profit organization formed to educate the public about the joys of butterfly observation, gardening, photography, and conservation.

Young Entomologists' Society, Inc.
6907 West Grand River Avenue
Lansing, MI 48906
http://insects.ummz./ lsa.umich.edu/YES/YES. html

An organization that provides publications and outreach programs for young people interested in insect study, including butterflies and moths. Its website includes a "Butterfly and Moth World" page.

45

Important Words

camouflage any disguise that hides or protects

cocoon covering spun by larvae of certain insects for protection during metamorphosis

compound made up of more than one part

generation group of living things born around the same time

mate to join together to produce offspring

metamorphosis process through which a caterpillar changes into an adult insect

pesticide poison

pheromone chemical substance produced by an animal to attract other animals of the same species

pupa insect in the stage of changing from a larva into an adult insect

species group of living things that are more or less alike

Index

Meet the Author

Larry Dane Brimner writes full-time for children. His other books about insects for Children's Press include *Bees*, *Cockroaches*, *Flies*, and *Praying Mantises*. In his spare time, he is an avid gardener and keeps a butterfly garden of his own.